:Spilling the Beans on...

MAKING IT IN

MUSIC

First published in 2001 by Miles Kelly Publishing,
Bardfield Centre, Great Bardfield, Essex CM7 4SL

Printed in Italy

ISBN 1-84236-010-8

24681097531

Cover design and illustration: Inc
Layout design: Mackerel

.

:Spilling the Beans on...

MAKING IT IN

MUSIC

by Nik Kershaw

Illustrations   Martin Remphry

Miles Kelly

PUBLISHING

Titles in the Series:
Making it in Football
Making it in Music
Making it in the Movies
Making it in the Ballet
Making it in the Fashion Industry
Making it in Computers

Contents

"For all those beautiful, talented people who didn't get lucky".

About the Author

Nik Kershaw is quite good at joined up writing. His works include a note to the milkman, a doodle on the back of a crisp packet and a limerick about a man from Steeple Bumpstead. He has absolutely no credentials for writing a children's book. On the other hand, he has had eleven top thirty, ten top twenty, six top ten and four top five hit singles as an artist, songwriter and producer; Platinum albums all over the world; and has been nominated for three Ivor Novello and four Brit Awards. So he might know something about the music business. He lives in Essex with his wife and three sons.

Triple Biology

It's Thursday afternoon and triple biology with Mr Yawn. He's banging on about rats' intestines and you're rapidly losing the will to live. There's another hour and a half of this. Don't know if you can take much more. Might have to fake a mystery stomach bug or something. Blame it on the school steak and kidney pie. Legendary in these parts. Surprised the World Health Organisation hasn't heard about it yet.

Mr Yawn's monotone ramblings fade into the distance as your attention is drawn outside to some builders working on the new gym block. The radio is on and you can just make out, drifting across the courtyard, the familiar strains of your favourite song. "Love and Porridge" by Conan Bleating. You suck the already soggy end of your HB pencil and stare dreamily out of the window.

Must be great to be a pop star. You think to yourself. *Aah, the glamour, the excitement, the money, the power, the adulation, the parties, the red carpet, the white limousines, the celebrity chums, the first-class travel, the five star hotels, the VIP lounges. Someone to open doors for you, someone to drive you about, someone to warm the toilet seat. And you don't even have to do any work. It must be fantastic!!*

Well, it is fantastic. Then again.......it isn't. I mean, like all things in life, it's a bit more complicated than that. The possible rewards are huge but

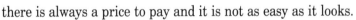

there is always a price to pay and it is not as easy as it looks.

So, what is it like being a pop star?

Don't ask me.

I wasn't, it was a rhetorical question and, in the pages that follow, I'm going to try to answer it for you. Not that I can tell you what it's like to be Robbie Williams or Britney Spears. Only they can tell you that. But, with the benefit of my experience (ask your mum), I can give you some idea what it might be like for a hypothetical pop star.

A what?

8

We're going to invent someone and follow him on his journey through the wacky world of the music business. On the way we'll meet some of the many characters involved in getting him to the top and, to make it all spookily real for you, we'll make you the aforementioned hypothetical popstar.

Eh?

Here we go:

Your name is Duncan Phillips.

No it's not, it's…

No, I know it's not but imagine, if you will, that you are Duncan Phillips, 16 years old from Wellard Garden City. You've been singing and writing your own songs since you were 11 and you eat, drink and sleep music. Your all-consuming dream is to play in front of tens of thousands of your adoring fans; to make multi-platinum, award-winning album after album; to light up the musical firmament with your own special kind of genius; to boldly go where no one h……

What if my real name is Sharon?

Good point! Although there are different issues and problems facing a girl in the music business, pretty much everything that follows is relevant to both sexes.

Oops, watch out, here comes your dad.

Your dad says: *"What's this I hear about you wanting to be* *a pop star? Ridiculous! Why can't you think of something sensible to do with your life? Get a good education. Then at least you'll have something to fall back on. The chances of you making it are one in a million."*

Of course, your dad's right, it is ridiculous, your chances *are* only one in a million, all sensible advice. But if you're going to go around taking sensible advice, then you're really not pop star material, are you? Besides, (and of this you have absolutely no doubt), you *are* one in a million.

So there you are, 18 years old...

I thought you said I was 16???

...and, having just achieved excellent grades in you're A levels (apart from biology, in which you were unable to answer a single question on rats' intestines), you're ready to take the first tenuous steps on the bumpy but well travelled road to mega stardom.

So you rush out and get a job in a carpet factory.

Mission Impossible

(Getting a Record Contract)

Before we proceed, please fill out this short questionnaire, just to make sure you're made of the right stuff.

---

1 Have you ever used a piece of sports equipment as a fantasy guitar?

2 Can you sleep standing up?

3 Your mates ask you out one evening for a game of football. Do you say:

a) Yes please, I'm in goal.

b) No thanks, I've got Geography revision to do.

c) No thanks, I've got to stay in and finish a song I'm writing.

d) Thank you for the kind offer dear friends but, on this occasion, I will have to regretfully decline as I have a large quantity of fluff to remove from my belly button.

---

4 Is your skin thicker than something that's really, really thick?

5 Do you think you're the best thing since disposable nappies?

6 Are you capable of looking cool and dignified while performing next to someone dressed as a giant chicken?

7 Are you good at sums?

Answers

1) Yes. You've got to dream the dream before you can live it.

2) Yes. This will come in useful when working 18-20 hour days.

3) c). (Or b), if your dad's reading this). Just checking to see how keen you are.

4) Yes. See Chapter 4 Making a splash: Get in the papers.

5) Yes. If you don't believe in yourself, no one else will

6) No. This is a trick question. No one is capable of looking cool and dignified whilst performing next to someone dressed as a giant chicken. Chapter 5 Rich and Famous.

7) Yes. You'll need to be good at sums to answer the following question: "Over the last three years I've sold 4,234,781 albums @ £12.99 each, 834,248 concert tickets @ £20 each and can't walk down the street without being set upon by 41.6 screaming girls. How come I'm still living in a council flat in Wapping?" Chapter 5 Rich and Famous.

We'll assume you scored at least 4/7.

One question not on the questionnaire is: Do you have any talent? This is a much more complicated question than it sounds. Some musical ability would seem to be a minimum requirement but, let's be honest, there are very successful stars out there with slightly less of it than your average fruit bat. This doesn't mean, however, that they are not talented.

It doesn't?

Their talents may lie in other areas, such as…

Such as?

…dancing, posing, communicating, smiling on cue, entertaining, looking good, performing under pressure, self promotion, getting out of limos….

These are talents?

…. or they may have none of these. They may just have…
'It'.

It?

'It', that certain, indefinable something that makes people reach for their autograph books; an unfathomable ability to walk into a room and, without even trying, immediately become the centre of attention; star quality, call it what you will,......'it'!

And do I, Duncan Phillips, have 'it' ?

Let's say you have a small quantity of it but could certainly do with some more. What you do have is a talent for song writing. You've a good, individual voice, you play a bit of guitar and you're not completely repulsive to the opposite sex.

Thank you very much!

My pleasure.

Get Noticed

Right, you've got your job in the carpet factory to keep you alive and we know what you're good at. So, what now? Do you:

a) hide in your bedroom and wait to be discovered?

b) show what you're good at to other people?

b) ?

Excellent. Of course, you **could** stay in your bedroom, practise your guitar, write the best song ever written, invent a car that runs on bath water and discover the meaning of life but, if no one else knows about it, it would be a bit pointless.

So get out there, show them what you're made of, put yourself about a bit, in other words... get noticed!

How?

Make A Demo

One way is to make a "demo" or demonstration tape/CD. This doesn't have to sound like a finished record but does need to be of good enough quality to get your ideas across. You don't need an expensive recording studio to do this. There are plenty of cheaper "demo" studios around. Also, home recording technology has come on leaps and bounds in recent years and, if you ask around, you can probably find someone with some decent equipment.

Don't go crazy! The biggest temptation when making your first recording is to go way over the top. Keep it simple, no showing off.

But I'm supposed to be showing off?

Well, yes but there's showing off and there's showing off! Keep to the point, steer clear of unnecessary embellishments or, if you want the technical term, twiddly bits.

If you're with a band, make sure you're well rehearsed before you get there. No point wasting valuable studio time working out arrangements. Put someone in charge to try and avoid the inevitable fight over whose twiddly bits should be the loudest.

WARNING: TOO MANY TWIDDLY BITS IMPRESS NO ONE!

Enough with the twiddly bits!

ANOTHER WARNING: EVERYTHING IN A STUDIO TAKES THREE AND A HALF TIMES LONGER THAN YOU THINK IT WILL!

There is Earth Time, and there is Studio Time.

For example:

"Hang on, I've just got to plug this in."

"How long will it take?"

"Ooh, five minutes."

5 minutes Studio Time = $17\frac{1}{2}$ minutes Earth Time.

So don't get too ambitious. Don't try and record too many songs in one go. Better to get two tracks sounding great than five sounding all right. "All right" won't be good enough to get you a record contract.

Play Some Gigs

It could help your cause if you've got a few concerts or "gigs" under your belt.

Gigging will give you a chance to hone your performing skills and build up a local fan base at the same time. You might want to give away/sell your new demo CD to these new fans.

Gigs are also great places to invite prospective managers, record company people but, probably, not your dad.

Get A Manager

It's possible to get a record deal without a manager but should be much easier with one. A good manager will know the business and how it works. He'll motivate you, suggest ways to improve your chances of success and he'll know all the right people.

Finding a good manager won't be easy. You won't find one in the yellow pages but you could try looking in a book called *The Music Week Directory*. In it you'll find names and addresses of record companies, publishing companies, recording studios, rehearsal studios, concert promoters and, most important to you, managers, along with the artists they manage.

Using this book, look for artists you admire and respect and find out who manages them. Then get on the phone and set up some meetings.

Why can't I just send my demo CD?

You could, but demo tapes and CDs have a habit of getting lost. They're put in huge piles along with other demos and,

---

*The Music Week Directory can be obtained from Miller Freeman Entertainment, 4th Floor, 8 Montague Close, London SE1 9UR. Tel: 020 7940 8500

eventually, filed in the wastepaper basket. A month later you'll be wondering why the person you sent it to hasn't called.

Is it because:

a) he's listened to your CD and thinks it's pants?

b) he's completely forgotten about your CD which is now propping up the wonky leg of his desk?

c) he's listened to your CD, thinks it's fantastic but is trapped under a giant root vegetable and can't get to the phone?

You'll never know unless you sit in his office and play the CD to him yourself, however nerve-wracking it is. Whatever the result, at least you'll know where you stand and that you've been listened to.

Make as many calls as you can. Fifty calls may result in ten appointments, which may result in one positive reaction. If you don't get anywhere, try fifty more. Don't be afraid of making a nuisance of yourself. Invite people to gigs, if they don't come, invite them again. Don't be put off by negative comments.

Alternatively, you may know someone already or you could try advertising in the music press. Don't be bashful, make sure the advert gets noticed. Maybe even...exaggerate a little.

> Multi-talented singer/songwriter seeks new management.
>
> Record company interest. Getting too big for current manager. No time wasters.

What record company? What current manager?

You're trying to hook a big manager. The bait should be nice and juicy. You're being creative.

I'm being dishonest!

This is no time to start having scruples. Once you've hooked him you can come clean.

You get four replies. Now you have to choose the right one. No pressure but this is the single most important decision you will make in your entire career.

And now, it's over to the Alhambra Ballroom, for the Duncan Phillips Manager pageant.

May we have the first contestant please.

Contestant 1.

Arthur is from Basildon. He's a successful, highly respected member of the local retailing community.

He's 48, 5'11", Capricorn, likes meeting people and selling them a car. He's a self-made man, has an impressive collection of Status Quo records (ask your dad) and now fancies getting into the music business. After all, how difficult can that be?

Contestant 2.

Lefty is from Peckham and has a brother who once knew George Michael's hairdresser's dentist.

He's 29, 5'6", Sagittarius, likes meeting people and getting them "sorted". He says he has many "contacts" in the business. He wears shades at night, gets very drunk, tells you you're going to be bigger than Elvis, then throws up on the fake Versace jacket he's just sold you.

Contestant 3.

Simon is from the Home Counties. He practised music business law for three years before setting up his own management company.

He's 36, 5'11", Taurus, likes meeting people and getting them to return his phone calls. He manages three other acts, including one you've actually heard of and he tells you he can't promise you anything but thinks you're great and would like to give it a shot.

Contestant 4.

Ed is from Blackpool. He's one of the top show business agents in the North West and wears a tie made from your granny's curtains.

He's 56, 4'10", Gemini, likes meeting people and getting them to buy him a drink. He thinks you're really going places and, if you'd just learn some Abba songs, he might be able to get you a spot supporting Dale Winton at the Assembly Rooms, Morecambe.

And the winner is:
Contestant number 3, Simon from the Home Counties.

(Fanfare, cheers, applause, contestants hug, Simon fights back tears of joy, walks shakily to front of stage holding ill-fitting crown on head with one hand and in the other, his prize, a three-year management contract with multi-talented singer/songwriter Duncan Phillips.)

Don't worry, he won't be wearing the bathing suit the next time you see him.

The Solicitor

This is probably a good time to talk about the legal side of things. Simon will be doing a lot on your behalf and wants to be sure you're not going to walk out on him once all the hard work is done. So, he asks you to sign the management contract he has in his hand.

I'll go and get my pen.

WARNING: DON'T SIGN ANYTHING!!

No?

Not until you've shown it to a solicitor, and I don't mean the one who helped your parents buy their house. I mean a solicitor who specialises in music and entertainment law. The aforementioned *Music Week Directory* will have listings of all the top firms. Choosing one is another matter. A bad solicitor or accountant is a bit like a dodgy curry... you don't find out until it's too late!

Go and see a few firms. Find out who you feel most comfortable with. In the coming years there'll be many legal matters you'll need advice on, so you could be entering a long-term relationship.

Solicitors are expensive but, as you don't have any money yet, most firms will sort out ways in which you can pay when you do.

The A&R Person

Having signed the contract, Simon wants to help you develop your skills a bit before going for a record deal. He may think you need a new demo, a more defined image or even a change of name.

Change of name?

Well, let's face it...Duncan Phillips, not exactly pop star sounding, is it?

Sounds all right to me!

Do Reginald Dwight and Gordon Sumner sound like pop stars?

Nope.

That's why they changed their names to Elton John and Sting, you see? Memorable.

Yeah, but there are plenty of pop stars with their real names!

There are, but Simon thinks you'll have a better chance if

you didn't sound like a second division footballer. Something punchy, something perky, something like... Duncan Donut.

That's a joke, right?

So, armed with your new name and freshly scrubbed behind the ears, you're ready to be taken to A&R.

A& what?

A&R stands for Artistes and Repertoire. This is left over from the 1950s, when the music business really got started. In those days singers rarely wrote their own songs so record companies employed A&R men to find the singers (Artistes) and then find the right songs for them (Repertoire). These days it's slightly different. A big part of the A&R person's job is dealt with in the following chapter. The part we're interested in here is the talent scout part.

Every major record company has an A&R department, consisting of several A&R persons. For example, at Unigramm Records, one of the larger fictitious companies, they have:

Zak. He's 19 and spends his nights flitting from one club/pub to another looking for the next big thing. He's streetwise, trendy, hungry, knows what's "happening", where it's "happening", who's making it "happen" and all before it actually 'happens'.

WARNING: THIS A&R PERSON WILL SELF DESTRUCT IN NINE MONTHS!!

Wally is 26 and has been with Unigramm for five years. He spends most of his time in his office working with the acts he's already signed. He'll go out at night to see a new band if he thinks it's worth his while and he knows what's "happening" but only just after it's actually happened.

Dave is 46 and has been doing this for twenty-seven years. He was responsible for signing many major acts in the late 70s and 80s but has done naff all since. He hasn't got a clue what's 'happening' or, for that matter, what day of the week it is. He lost the ability to walk and chew gum simultaneously in 1986 due to an excess of "consciousness expanding" drugs.

All the above operate under the guidance of **Julian**, the head of A&R. He has the final word on whether an act gets signed or not. He also personally looks after two of the company's most important and longest serving artistes. He's not too up on what's "happening" but makes sure he employs staff who are. (Excluding Dave, obviously.)

One of Simon's other acts is with Unigramm so he knows Wally and Julian pretty well. This is his first call. He meets with Wally and plays him a couple of tracks from your CD. Wally says he'd like to meet you and hear some more.

A week later you walk into the chrome and wood panelled reception of Unigramm Records Inc. You're escorted down Platinum Disc lined corridors to the A&R department and, finally, into Wally's office. Tapes and CDs cover his desk, half the furniture, and a fair bit of the floor. Unread faxes cover the rest.

Simon makes the introductions. Wally is very friendly, offers you coffee, small talk, how are things, lousy weather, Arsenal back four etc and then down to business.

Three tracks are played, during which time Simon listens intently and Wally leans back in his chair, chews his pen, picks his nose, looks out of the window, reads two faxes, answers three phone calls and orders his lunch.

Simon stops the CD and there's an eerie silence, a bit like after one of your Dad's jokes.

"Interesting", says Wally and, looking at Simon, "We'll talk."

More chat, how's the family, did you see so and so on telly, see you soon and, before you know it, you're out on the street hailing a cab.

"What do you think?" you ask Simon.

"Plenty more fish in the sea", he says.

Indeed, during the next six months you get to go fishing for most of them. There's Dan at Polygon Records, Sophie at Pacific Records, Jim at M.F.I. Records and Nobby at Totally Skint Records. Dan & Jim have told Simon to come back when there's more material and Sophie and Nobby are non committal. When asked what they think Sophie says "Er" and Nobby says "Um". This is why the A&R department is sometimes referred to as the "Um & Er" department.

Publishing Companies

Now would be a good time to mention publishing companies.

Go on then!

If you write or co-write your own songs you'll need a publisher. A publisher registers your songs with collection agencies worldwide. These agencies collect an amount of money, called a "royalty", every time one of your records is sold. They then send the money to your publisher who keeps a percentage and passes the rest on to you.

Why are we talking about collecting royalties on records? I haven't even got a record contract.

A publisher could help you get one. They'll have relationships with all the top record companies and might be able to pull some strings. Besides, at some point you might want to write songs for other people and they can help you with that.

And a publishing contract is easy to get?

Not easy, but easier than a record contract. If you look as though you've got some chance of a successful recording career, a publisher will jump at the chance of signing you and, if they sign you now, they'll get you cheap. If they wait until you've got a record deal, they'll have to join in a massive bidding war with all the other major publishers.

As you're having problems getting a record deal, Simon decides to sign you to Condor Music Publishing now. You get a modest advance. (An advance is money paid to you when you sign. You won't get any royalties until this is paid back.) This means you can afford to give up your job at the carpet factory and concentrate on music. They'll pay you a 70% royalty (not bad, not good) and the term of the agreement is three albums or five years, whichever is sooner.

Is that good?

It's not great but you're in no position to be choosy at the moment. If you have some success, you may be able to renegotiate the deal.

And if I don't?

Back to the carpet factory.

The Showcase Gig

Eleven months have passed since you first met Simon. With the money you got from Condor you've bought some home recording equipment and have been beavering away writing new songs and recording demos. Simon has taken you to see twelve more Um & Er people and gone back to the ones you saw before. Wally at Unigramm, Sophie at Pacific and Nobby at Totally Skint seem a bit more interested this time but none of them has offered you a deal.

I'm getting a little disillusioned.

Don't worry. This is all perfectly normal. Never let anyone tell you getting a record contract is easy.

Simon suggests putting on a showcase. This is where you hire a trendy bar or club for the evening and play a gig. There'll be free food and drink and Simon has invited Wally, Sophie, Nobby and five other A&R persons. The theory is they'll all see each other there, think that everybody's after you and sign you quick before somebody else does. Invite all your mates and as many of your fans as you can press gang (an offhand mention of the free food and drink might be appropriate) and instruct them to be as enthusiastic as possible.

Sounds expensive.

Yes, but Condor have agreed to put up the money. After all, they've got as much to gain from it as anyone.

The big night arrives. You play a storming 40 minutes...

Is that all?

Any more and an A&R person's attention will start wandering. Probably already seen two bands tonight and the free drinks are beginning to kick in. Best to leave them wanting more.

Everybody has a great time and staggers home happy. The next morning you meet Simon. He has good news and bad news.

What's the bad news?

Only Wally and Nobby actually turned up...

Oh.

....and Nobby disappeared into the toilets after two songs and hasn't been seen since.

Ah, and the good news?

Someone at Condor has been talking to Wally...

Yes?

...and Simon's been talking to Julian at Unigramm.

Yes?

...and they want to do a deal.

Yes!!!!!!

Of course, it could happen a lot easier than that or it could be a lot harder. Let me demonstrate with this cunningly devised board game:

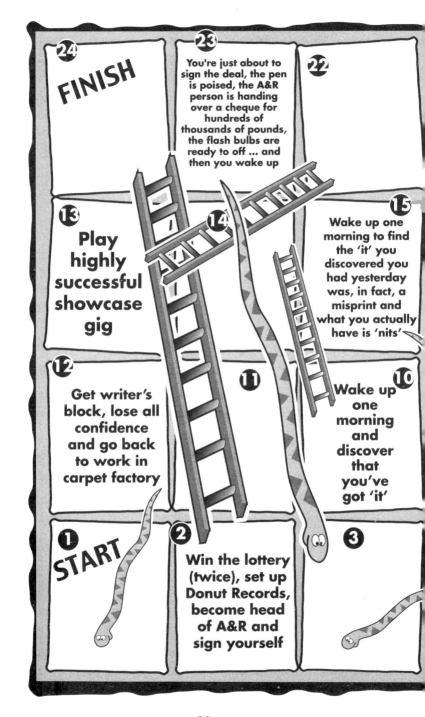

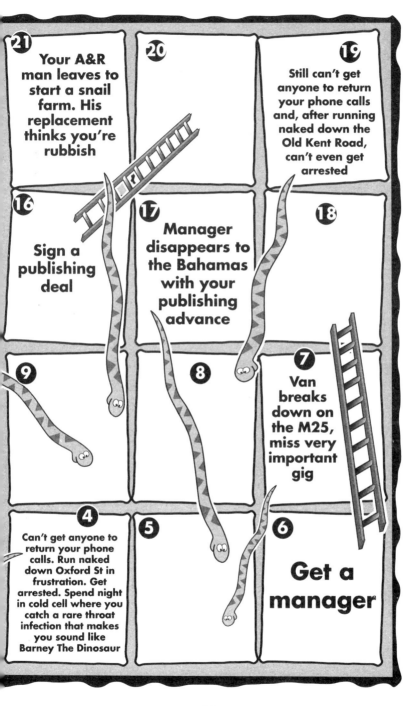

21 Your A&R man leaves to start a snail farm. His replacement thinks you're rubbish

20

19 Still can't get anyone to return your phone calls and, after running naked down the Old Kent Road, can't even get arrested

16 Sign a publishing deal

17 Manager disappears to the Bahamas with your publishing advance

18

9

8

7 Van breaks down on the M25, miss very important gig

4 Can't get anyone to return your phone calls. Run naked down Oxford St in frustration. Get arrested. Spend night in cold cell where you catch a rare throat infection that makes you sound like Barney The Dinosaur

5

6 Get a manager

There seem to be rather more snakes than ladders?

And so, four months later, after intensive negotiations, you sign a rather large cheque to your solicitor and a three-album record contract with Unigramm Records Incorporated.

Congratulations. Go out and celebrate, the big time is just around the corner. Order the Ferrari, your troubles are over, sorted. Right?

Er, no.

Baking The Cake

(Making the Record)

A & R (Again)

Wally's done the first part of his job, the talent scout part.
Now he's responsible for getting the record made or, at least
getting other people to make it.

How much input he has depends on what kind of artist you
are and how much help you'll actually need. If you fit the
typical artist's profile you won't think you'll need any. If he fits
the typical A&R man's profile, he'll want to get involved in
everything. This is quite often the cause of artist/A&R man
fisticuffs.

Let's assume you're both reasonable people and your
relationship proceeds as follows: He helps you choose the
right producer.

What's a producer?

We'll get to that in a minute.

Unigramm are putting up the money (don't worry, you'll pay in the end) so he'll want to make sure it's spent wisely. He helps you and the producer choose the songs and then decide the best way to record them.

The Songs

Wally thought your songs were good enough to sign you, but thinks you could do with a couple more "smash hits" before you start on the album. He offers you the following options:

a) Write the songs yourself (collect all the writer's royalty).

b) Get someone to write them for you (collect none of the royalty).

c) Write them with someone else (collect half of the royalty).

d) Sit in the same room as someone writing the songs whilst you try to think of a rhyme for banana/play with your Game Boy/talk on the phone/pluck your eyebrows/take a nap (also half the royalty).

e) Record a cover version (an old song, probably a big hit your mum can sing along with).

Note: Options d) and e) have proved surprisingly popular with boy/girl bands in recent years.

Every now and then you'll have A&R meetings involving you, Simon, a producer and Charlie. (Sorry, I forgot to mention, Charlie is your new A&R man. Wally is now head of marketing at M.F.I. Records.) The purpose of these meetings is to check how things are going, play all the new songs and formulate your career plan for the coming months. Typical comments during one of these meetings would be:

☆ "Wow, great song."

☆ "Sounds like a hit to me."

☆ "Yeah, I think we're really headed in the right direction."

☆ "I'll have the lobster, please, and a nice dry white wine."

This last comment is more likely if the meeting takes place at Charlie's favourite restaurant. This differs slightly from the other kind of A&R meeting. No music is played and the conversation might stray to football. Charlie gets to use the company's gold credit card and you get to hear how fab you are.

Both meetings end the same way. The producer says he's really excited to be involved with the project and, as soon as he's finished with Robbie Williams/The Snot Wrestlers/Elvis (place name of choice here), he wants to get started. You feel like the centre of the universe and scurry home to write another hit song, which you play to everybody at the next A&R meeting. Typical comments during one of these meetings would be:

☆ "Wow, great song"

☆ "Sounds like…etc, etc."

<u>WARNING:</u> THIS PROCESS CAN TAKE SEVERAL YEARS!

(And I'm not exaggerating.)

The Recording Studio

The meetings are over, the songs have been chosen and you're sitting in the control room at Farmyard Studios surrounded by hundreds of thousands of pounds worth of recording equipment.

You're ready to record your first album.

Rogues Gallery

Here's a brief rundown of some of the people you might bump into in a recording studio:

☞ Chris, the producer

There are many different kinds of producer. Some are very "hands on" and like to do everything themselves, whereas some don't do anything but know plenty of people who do.

Either way, the producer is responsible for the day to day process of making the record.

He has an almost impossible job. Charlie, Simon, Julian, the head of Unigramm, Chris's manager, your mum, the milkman, the milkman's manager (oh yes, and you), will all have an opinion as to how the record should sound and it's up to the producer to keep everybody happy.

A good producer would be able to do any of the following jobs: politician, army general, football referee, road sweeper.

Not all artists use a producer, they will co-produce or produce it themselves, but Unigramm are unlikely to trust their investment to somebody with as little studio experience as you.

☞ Ben, the engineer

Some engineers work for the studio. Ben doesn't, he's freelance and can work anywhere and for anyone he likes.

Remember the hundreds of thousands of pounds worth of recording equipment I mentioned? Ben knows how to use all of it. Every knob, switch and fader. If you or Chris say to him, "I want this to sound like a one-legged man hitting a traffic cone with a haddock", he'll know exactly which machine to use and what setting to put it on.

He's Chris's right-hand man and Chris relies on him for a second opinion. They make a great team and seem to speak a secret language you don't understand. Don't worry, within weeks you'll be speaking it fluently.

☞ Penny, the studio manager

Penny's job is to book the studios, deal with the record companies and generally make sure everything is running smoothly. A large studio complex could have as many as five different studios. Everybody who works for the studio answers to her. She's probably quite good at shouting. (Don't worry, not at you, she'll make sure you have everything your little heart desires.)

☞ Bob, the maintenance engineer

Bob's a bit of a boffin. He uses words like "Digital clock rate" and "Ohms". If he talks to you just nod and pretend you know/care what he's on about. He wears jeans your dad wouldn't be seen dead in and a lumberjack shirt. His skin is the colour of those frogs you find in caves and he always looks as though he's just got out of bed, which is rather surprising considering he never actually goes to bed. He's on call 24 hours a day, just in case something goes wrong with the equipment. (Something usually does.) The time lost due to breakdowns is called "Down Time" and it's up to Chris to make sure Penny doesn't charge you for it. This is quite often the cause of producer/studio manager fisticuffs.

☞ Nigel, the assistant engineer

Nigel's job description is too long to go into in detail, but can be summed up as: anything nobody else wants to do. He

makes tea, gets sandwiches,
labels tapes, organises hire
equipment, tidies the studio,
laughs at everybody's jokes, is
the first to arrive and the last
to leave. Oh yes, and he assists
the engineer, which means
carrying/setting up gear,
plugging things in and taking
the blame for all his mistakes
whilst learning the noble art of

sound recording. All for slightly less money than a paper
round. If you want to work in a recording
studio, this is where you start.

☞ Tony, the chef

Most major studio complexes
have their own café/restaurant.
You can waste a whole lot of time
and energy sorting out food every
day, so it's really handy having it all
done for you.

Tony's quite a character. He can make a Bacon, Lettuce
and Tomato sandwich with one hand while scratching his rash
with the other. He has an opinion on any subject (the opposite
of yours) and his middle name is Surly but he does know how
Madonna likes her eggs so even Penny won't shout at him.

☞ Doris, the cleaning lady

Doris comes in at 7.00 every morning. If you're seeing a lot of her it means one of two things:

a) You are very, very keen and have arrived early.

b) It really is time you were in bed.

Brief Outline Of The Recording Process

The first thing to understand is that there is no such thing as a brief outline of the recording process.

Aah!

This is because there are as many ways to make a record as there are lumps in school custard. You can spend a quarter of a million pounds in the studio complex above or a few hundred in your bedroom. (Although you might want to tidy it first.)

A lot depends on what type of music you do. Some dance or garage acts, for instance, will do most of their work on computers in small, cheap or home studios and use a big studio for the finishing touches. A rock band is more likely to spend all of its time in the big studio.

You might want to use digital hard disk or analogue multi-track.

Excuse me?

You might want to record everything live or start with the rhythm track and overdub on top of it.

What are you on about?

You might want to have a herd of wildebeest doing the Charleston whilst you play the tuba in a bucket full of jelly.

Eh?

What I'm saying is, if this book was called "Spilling the beans on making a record", I could spend the next three hundred pages banging on about everything that could happen in a recording studio. But it's not, so I won't.

Phew!

Mixing

Now you've finished all the recording, you'll want to mix the record.

I will?

Up to now, you've been listening to your songs on expensive, state of the art "multi-track" recording equipment.

I have?

Unfortunately, not many people have recording studios in their front rooms so, to enable people to play it on their stereos, you have to "mix" it down to two tracks: the left and right side of the stereo.

This consists of tweaking and polishing the individual instruments and sounds then balancing them together until your humble song couldn't possibly sound any better.

As this is the final act in the recording process, the good people at Unigramm have suddenly become very interested. In fact, after not seeing them for three months, you can't seem to get rid of them. Charlie's there, Julian's there, Simon's there. Charlie wants the voice louder, Julian wants the drums louder and Simon seems to want everything louder than everything else.

Chris remains remarkably cool, acting on each request with theatrical abandon, twisting a knob here, pushing a fader there and humbly acknowledging each suggestion, however ridiculous, as the best idea since the Pot Noodle. Four hours later everybody leaves happy and you listen, bewildered, to something that sounds exactly the same as it did before they arrived.

Anyway, everybody's happy so the "mix" is recorded onto a stereo tape machine.

So that's it then!

Well, almost. Now you have to get the record "cut".

Cut?

Yes, you take the tape with your stereo mix on it to a "Cutting Suite" where a "Cutting Engineer" "cuts" it.

Thank you, that's much clearer.

It's the process you go through before sending it to the CD pressing factory. The cutting engineer listens to all of your songs and makes tiny little adjustments to the overall sound. People won't want to be constantly adjusting their stereos so he makes sure all the songs are the same kind of volume and have the same amount of bass and treble on them. The engineer also "compiles" the album, which means putting all the songs in order and making sure all the gaps between are right. He puts a special coded message at the beginning of each song so your CD player will know how to find its way around.

The final tape (or PQ'd master) is then sent off to the CD factory where they make a thing called the "Glass Master", from which all the CDs are pressed.

So, that's it then.

Well, almost. It's at this point that Charlie sends the song that is to be the first single, to be remixed.

But everybody's happy with the mix, I mean, they were there, they said it sounded great.

And so it does but you're going to need a dance mix for the clubs, a garage mix, a garden shed mix, an ambient mix, a not so ambient mix, a pick & mix and maybe a special radio mix. He sends a tape with just the vocal (your singing) on it to Todd Flava the coolest, hippest, trendiest, most ludicrously expensive remixer on the planet.

Todd takes your vocal, chooses the bits he likes, throws away the bits he doesn't, speeds it up, stretches it out, turns it backwards, forwards, sideways and puts it through an effect that makes you sound like a chipmunk in a tumble dryer.

He then creates his own drums, bass, keyboards and backing sounds to go with it. These might be in the same key as the vocal.

The end result is "pumpin" and "wickid", apparently.

These mixes can be used to send to club DJs; as bonus tracks on the CD single; or to wedge open an old sash window.

And so your first single "Cloud Cuckoo" is recorded, mixed, cut and is rolling off the CD presses as we speak.

So, that's it then?

So that's it then.

Making A Splash
(Promoting The Record)

You've poured your heart and soul into making a record. Several torturous months of intensive toil have resulted in 64 minutes of pure magic; a Big Mac and Fries for the ears; a landmark in popular music; let's not be bashful, a masterpiece.

That's the easy bit!

Now you've got to let the world know about it.

I feel a statistic coming on:

There are, on average, about 200 singles and 500 albums released in the UK every week.

So, if you're going to get your record noticed, you'll have to put yourself about a bit.

Putting Yourself About A Bit.

The photo session

You arrive at a converted warehouse in Battersea with a song in your heart, a spring in your step and all your best togs stuffed into a couple of Tesco carrier bags.

You're greeted by Andy, the photographer's assistant. Then Lucy, your make-up artist for the day, Terrance the photographer and Joanne.............. **The Stylist!!!**

The what?

Up to now you thought you looked ok, huh? I mean you've been dressing yourself since your were what, five or so? Tying your own shoelaces and everything, right?

Right!

Well that's just not good enough, so Joanne's been hired by Unigramm. It's their subtle way of telling you "we love your music, we think you're great but, let's be honest, you look rubbish!" She's mid to late twenties, impossibly thin and thinks she's your mum. Joanne was never allowed to play with dolls when she was a kid so, as you'll come to realise, you're Barbie.

"So what have we got here then, darling?"

First, she rifles through your Tesco bags, holding each of your beloved items up to the light, gingerly between thumb and forefinger, whilst muttering things like,

"mmmm, unusual colour" and

"these used to be all the rage, didn't they?"

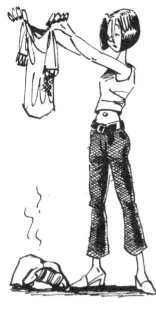

Meanwhile, Lucy has unpacked her creams and potions onto the table. She sits you down in front of the mirror and stands behind you, thoughtfully tousling your hair. It's like being at the hairdresser's but, instead of asking where you're going for your holiday, she asks,

"Have you tried this new spot cream?"

So, with your self esteem around your ankles, Joanne and Lucy begin to work their magic.

<u>WARNING:</u> YOU'RE ABOUT TO GET STYLED!

Joanne has also brought some carrier bags but, rather than Tesco, they have Versace, Paul Smith and Dolce & Gabanna printed on them.

Ooh, lovely clothes and all for me?

BANG!!!

What was that?

That was a myth being exploded. All those great clothes you see pop stars wearing in photographs and videos? They probably don't actually own most of them. Joanne borrows or hires them from shops and takes them back when the session's over. When you've sold a few hundred thousand records you might think about keeping some but, at the moment, that shirt you're wearing costs more than your car.

After an hour of tousling, preening, moisturising, powdering, crimping, plucking, gelling, painting and plastering, you're ready for the session to begin. The miracle has been worked, they've transformed this plain, ordinary person into someone really special; someone who'll stand out from the crowd; someone who'll turn heads and stop traffic. In short... you look completely ridiculous.

"Wow, you look completely amazing", says Joanne.

"Really cool", says Lucy.

Andy and Tarquin have set up the cameras, a smoke machine and some moody lighting. You step up apprehensively and strike one of the poses you've been practising in front of the mirror for the last ten years.

"Yep, yep, that's great; *click* now, look at the camera; *click* super, left hand on your right knee; *click* nice, right hand behind your head; right, last one (this is a lie!); *click* fantastic and left foot in your right ear; marvellous and hold it there and... smile! *Click*! OK, I'm just going to shoot some black and white, *click* x 24, great now let's try another set up."

Change of clothes, patch up your make up, reconstruct your hair and do it all again, and again. Anywhere from two to ten hours later you're ready to drop. You hurt in places you didn't even know you had places and your face feels like someone's been gardening on it, but you wend your weary way home happy, armed with several Polaroids of you looking, it has to be said, a bit like a pop star.

Note: *These photographs can be used to amuse your mates and, in later life, to frighten your children.*

Make A Video

During the course of the next few months you'll be required to be in seventeen different places at the same time. If you have a video, you can be.

Several video directors are contacted, sent a copy of "Cloud Cuckoo" and asked for their ideas. They all submit a short synopsis, or "treatment", outlining their vision for the song.

A treatment might look something like this:

Freeze Frame Productions

Director: Albert Hitchcock

Producer: Louise B Mayer

Artist: Duncan Donut

Treatment for **"Cloud Cuckoo"**

Opening scene: Sunrise on a deserted beach somewhere in the Bahamas. Intro of song starts. We pan with Duncan as he walks slowly along the shoreline. He's dressed in white flannel, barefooted and lost in deep thought. Suddenly his attention is caught by movement to his left.

Cut to beautiful girl appearing from the waves. She's dressed in bikini bottoms and short, torn T-shirt.

Sounds pretty good so far.

Cut back to Duncan singing the opening line of the song: "I saw my baby walking down the street."

Cut to interior of space ship. It is dark. Moody lighting, water streaming down the walls. Duncan floats by wearing a tutu made from tinfoil singing (in slow motion) "She had two pink eyes and three webbed feet."

Fade to special effects, explosions, intergalactic car chase, zoom in on one of the cars, Duncan is driving, the girl from the first scene is sitting beside him, running her fingers through his hair. "The way she moves is supersonic."

Cut to New York, Duncan riding a unicycle on top of Empire State Building. Zoom out from the helicopter as he sings: "Mine's a pork pie and a gin and tonic."

Street scene, carnival time in Rio, thousands of bizarrely attired extras singing chorus: "Cloud Cuckoo Zoo, Cloud Cuckoo Zoo, I'd give my entire Pokemon card collection for just one night with you."

Fade to yacht in South of France, more beautiful girls…. blah, blah…. bikinis….. blah….. dancing frogs…. etc, etc.

Estimated cost: £392, 428.17p

How much?

Meetings follow between you, Unigramm, Simon and the

prospective directors. You tell everybody your ideas and the director scribbles them down in a notepad.

Note: *These will be completely ignored.*

A decision is made and you're off to shoot a video with Albert Hitchcock and Freeze Frame Productions.

Excellent! I'll go and get my passport.

Erm, as our budget is only £20,000, we've had to make a few minor adjustments.

The Bahamas, New York, Rio?

A disused railway shed in Docklands.

The special effects, the beautiful girls?

A box of old fireworks and they might be able to get that woman from Eastenders. But we can still afford the tinfoil tutu so don't worry, it's going to look great. Albert said so.

The video shoot itself is a bit like the photo session except with more jumping about. Joanne and Lucy are there along with about fifty other people. What do they all do? Here are a few key characters:

☞ Albert, director

He's in charge. He tells everybody what to do and when to

do it. He went to art school for three years and he thinks he's Steven Spielberg. He's written a shooting script which he follows religiously until shot 3 when he starts making it up as he goes along.

☞ Louise, producer

She deals with Unigramm and calculates the budget. She hires the people Albert wants and fires the people he doesn't. She's here today to make sure the money is being spent wisely and to sort out any last minute problems. She's constantly whispering in Albert's ear. Things like: "We're running out of time" and "Where are we going to find a giant bowl of porridge this time of night?"

☞ Don, lighting cameraman

Don knows how to get Albert's grand vision onto film. He operates the camera and organises the lighting. He has something that looks like a small telescope around his neck which he keeps looking at you through. He also has a light meter which

tells him how much light there is. From this he works out the correct settings for the camera.

☞ Gail, focus puller

CLOUD CUCKOO
TAKE 47

Gail is Don's assistant. As you have quite a small budget, she's doing several people's jobs today. She loads the camera, labels all the different rolls of film and marks the clapperboard at the beginning of each shot. She also changes the focus on the camera during the shot. If the camera is on a track or rails, she helps move the camera about.

☞ Calvin, sparks

That's Calvin up that ladder. Don thinks it's too dark in the corner and it's Calvin's job to move the lights around until he's happy. He's responsible for anything electrical on the set.

☞ Phil, chippy

Give Phil an old-washing up-liquid bottle, and a rusty nail and he'll give you a full scale, working model of the *Titanic*. He can make or fix anything. He'll spend the day banging, sawing, drilling, sticking, building any piece of scenery Albert requires.

☞ Ian, gopher

If Albert needs some toenail clippers at two o'clock in the

morning, Ian will run out and get them. He's called a "gopher" because, during the course of the day, he'll be asked to "gopher" (go for) toilet paper, "gopher", batteries, drill bits, film, Albert's laundry, a hub cap for a 1986 Vauxhall Viva and, of course, tinfoil.

☞ Choice Cuts, catering

Ian's going to be pretty busy all day, so he won't have time to run out and get 36 lamb curries, 23 vegetable lasagnes, 16 fish & chips, 27 ham rolls (14 with mustard), 17 chicken salad sandwiches, 19 cheese and tomato pitta breads, 3 vegeburgers, 31 donuts (12 jam, 9 cream, 8 chocolate and 2 pigeon), 197 teas (88 with sugar), 213 coffees, 246 cans of cola and a packet of Polos. Choice Cuts are a mobile catering company specialising in the film and music business.

☞ Eduardo, head of wardrobe

Joanne will be personally seeing to your fashion needs (lucky you) but Eduardo will be looking after all the extras. He's got Louis XIV, Henry VIII,  dancing girls, Spanish revolutionaries, a pantomime horse and a talking tree to dress and two assistants to help him do it. His very special friend Quentin will be doing their make-up.

☞ **Linda, sound**

She's in charge of playback. That is, when you're performing your song, you'll need something to sing along with. So, when the video is put together, your mouth movements are in time to the music. This is called "Lip-synch". Linda makes sure the tape is always in the right place and ready when Albert is.

☞ **Extras**

You, of course, are the star of this video but you'll need extra people to be in crowd scenes or to take supporting roles. Most of these will probably be your mates. (They may not be any good, but they'll do it for a laugh and a bacon sandwich.) The people playing the important parts come from an acting agency. The back end of the pantomime horse spends all day relating humorous anecdotes about his famous "old friends".

It's 6.30 in the morning, freezing cold, catering's doing a roaring trade in strong black coffee and Albert wants Lucy to get your make-up on so you'll be ready when he is. Albert shouts, Don squints, Louise chats on the mobile, Phil saws, Calvin plugs things in, Ian runs about a bit and, by 10.15, they're ready to go. Meanwhile, you've drunk seven cups of coffee, eaten two boxes of Jammy Dodgers, had three changes of make-up and tried on everything in Joanne's carrier bags. Twice!!

"Number ones," shouts Albert. (Director's speak for

"everybody get in your starting positions.") "Roll camera."

"Speed", says Don. (This means the camera is up to speed.)

"Sound", says Albert and Linda starts the tape. "And....
Action!"

This part of the video will be for the second verse and the last chorus but Albert gets you to sing the whole song just in case he wants to use it somewhere else.

Take 1: You perform it brilliantly. Every little hand gesture is just right and you even manage to pull off that little eyebrow movement you've been practising in front of the mirror. Unfortunately, Don spotted a bit of glare he didn't like so you'll have to do it again.

Take 2: You're not quite as good but, don't worry, one of the extras fell over a lighting cable so you'll get another go.

Take 3: Even better than the first one except Gail didn't get the focus pulled on cue. One more time.

Take 4: Everything runs smoothly. Don's happy, Albert's

happy and all the extras were magnificent. Unfortunately, your make-up was starting to crack, you forgot the words and that little eyebrow movement went horribly wrong, making you look like a startled chimp.

"Great, that's the one", says Albert, "Next set-up." Frantic activity ensues. Scenery is torn down, cameras are reloaded, lights are moved ready for the next shot. You're whisked off to have your make-up replenished and to be squeezed into that tinfoil tutu.

"But, but, but…", says you.

This continues until about two o'clock the next morning, by which time you've performed the song 673 times. The only thing keeping your eyes open is the twelve layers of make-up you've accumulated and you wish you'd never written the stupid song. You've just finished the last word of the last chorus of the last take.

"That's a rap", announces Albert to cheers and applause. Elation drifts over you and all you can think about is a nice, warm, comfortable bed. "Check the gate", you hear Albert say as you wander off in a contented daze. You don't know what this means and, quite frankly, you don't care.

"Hair in the gate", shouts Gail, and a tired groan goes up around the set. She's found a small piece of fluff between the camera lens and the film. You're going to have to do that last shot all over again.

About a week later you all meet at Unigramm to view the finished video. Albert's been working away in a film editing suite until the small hours and is ready to show you his finished masterpiece.

Whilst you're all watching, Albert proudly explains to you how he got that subtle lighting effect on the pantomime horse. The tape finishes.

"Fantastic", says Charlie.

"Excellent", says Simon.

"What has that got to do with my song? What happened to all my ideas? Where's the bit we spent three hours shooting with me and Louis XIV? Why did you keep the bit where I look like a startled chimp?" says you.

Get In The Papers

Enter Ken, your press agent. Unigramm has its own press department but, as you're so special, they've agreed to pay for an independent agent.

Ken used to work for a national tabloid so he knows all the right people and tricks of the trade. Beware, he'll do anything to get you in the papers, because:

"All publicity is good publicity!"

BANG!!!

Another myth?

Yeth, I mean yes. It's true, there have been cases of dreadful publicity boosting someone's career but there are more cases of it destroying one. Anyway, just because a bit of sensational gossip may sell a few more records, it won't necessarily be good for **you**. You might not want everybody on the planet to know you wear Telly Tubby boxer shorts and have a cuddly toy rabbit called Nigel, for instance.

How did you know…?

It was in yesterday's papers. A journalist was buying one of your best mates some drinks and squeezed a few bits of juicy inside information out of him.

What? What else did he…?

Oh, nothing much but, if you're wondering why your girlfriend isn't returning your calls….

This is terrible!!!

Not really, you'll sell loads more records. After all, who needs friends and loved ones when you can jump a couple more chart positions.

Note: a good press agent will put as much effort into keeping you out of the papers as he will getting you into them.

Ken will sit you down and ask you to tell him the story of your life, paying special attention to those exciting and newsworthy bits. Every newspaper will want an angle, something that makes your story special. It's no use them saying "Here's a picture of Duncan Donut. He's got a new record." You'll need to give them a good headline.

What if there isn't anything?

There's always something. Let's see, have you ever had any near death experiences?

I once fell off my bike and grazed my knee!

There you go, I can see the headlines now, let me get my typewriter:

DUNCAN'S DICE WITH DEATH.
DUNCAN DONUT SPEAKS FOR THE FIRST TIME OF HIS HORRIFIC MOTORCYCLE ACCIDENT.

Er, it was a push bike, I was 7.

Let's not split hairs. Any traumatic relationship break-ups?

I was quite upset when Tracy left to go to a different school.

Fantastic!

DONUT FORSAKE ME OH MY DARLING!
DUNCAN IS SUNK WITHOUT A TRACY!

Any exciting hobbies?

Not really, haven't got time, too busy...

Never mind, we'll just have to get a little bit 'creative'.

You don't mean...tell fibs?

Like I said, Ken used to work for a national tabloid.

He'll put everything he's learnt from your little chat into a short biography which he'll then send out to all the journalists.

Interviews

At first, Ken will be scraping around for any interview he can get. You're not exactly hot stuff yet. Maybe a couple of freelance journalists have expressed an interest and there's a bloke from the *Angling Times* on the phone but the dailies will be less than enthusiastic to start with.

However, let's assume you've already had a fair bit of success and Ken has organised some interviews at a posh London hotel. You arrive at 10.00 and the first interview is at 10.30. There are eighteen today at half hourly intervals. Among them are journalists from two daily newspapers, two lifestyle magazines, three teen magazines, two "serious" music papers and one 'Lads" magazine. You'll have an hour for lunch.

Angela, who works for Ken, is waiting for you with plenty of coffee and sandwiches. She'll be bringing the journalists in and out making sure no one goes over time.

First on is Norman Dempsey from *The Daily Enquirer*. Angela brings him in, introduces you, offers him a drink and leaves you to it. You both make yourselves comfortable and Norman gets out his dictaphone to tape the interview.

Norman: So, Duncan, love the new record.

You: Thanks a lot.

Norman: Did it take long?

You: The whole album took about four months. Some late nights at the end.

Norman: Really? What did your girlfriend think about that?

You: Uh, I'm in between girlfriends at the moment.

Norman: Young, free and single, eh?

You: Something like that.

Norman:	You must have plenty of offers.
You:	(Joking) Ooh, hundreds. The girls can't keep their hands off me. (Laugh).
Norman:	What do you do to relax?
You:	I do like to put my feet up with a good book and nice long walks in the country.
Norman:	It says in your biography that you like hang-gliding, snowboarding and "partying like there's no tomorrow".
You:	It does? Ah yes well, you know, when I'm not reading a good book and walking in the country…

The 30 minutes whiz by and Angela comes to collect Norman. He rises, picks up his dictaphone, shakes your hand and heads for the door.

WARNING: THE DICTAPHONE HAS NOT BEEN SWITCHED OFF!!

You're relaxing with a nice cool drink. Norman turns and speaks:

"Off the record, have you heard that new Snot Wrestler's single? Isn't it appalling? Can't believe those deaf idiots at Radio 1 are playing it!"

WARNING: THERE IS NO SUCH THING AS "OFF THE RECORD"!!

You: (Not wishing to offend) Yeah, right. Dreadful.

Norman: Anyway, best of luck, bye!

Well, he seemed like a nice bloke.

Mmmm, he did, didn't he. Let's fast forward to tomorrow. You pick up the early edition of *The Daily Enquirer* and turn to Norman Dempsey's page.

DUNCAN DONUT SLAMS THE SNOT WRESTLERS!

Eh?

In an astonishing outburst yesterday, Duncan Donut attacked the nation's favourite band, The Snot Wrestlers. He said the new single was *"dreadful"*.

"Isn't it appalling? Can't believe those deaf idiots at Radio 1 are playing it."

---

*I didn't say that, **he** did!!*

He doesn't say you did.

But it looks as though I did.

I did warn you!

Not content with insulting our heroes, the arrogant Donut went on to claim that he could have the pick of "hundreds" of girls. "They can't keep their hands off me," he said.

I was joking! He knew that.

Four and a half million readers think you were serious.

Are all the interviews going to be like this?

Of course not, some will be worse.

Aaaaarrrgh!!

But most will be better. There will be journalists who are genuinely interested in what you're doing and will do their best to relate this to their readers; there'll be those who don't care for what you do but will write responsibly and intelligently about you; and there will be those who, although well meaning, are just not very good at their job.

How do I tell the difference?

While you're talking to them? You can't. Just be on your guard at all times.

So, back to the day's interviews. From No.5 onwards, a strange thing starts happening. Your mouth starts answering the questions with very little help from your brain. This is because they're the same questions you've answered four times already. By interview No.10 you can answer the question: "What's the new song about?", whilst simultaneously calculating the square root of 497.

9.30pm and it's all over, for today at least. There'll be many more days like this. Also, you'll find yourself fitting in interviews left, right and centre. At the TV studio, photo session, on the phone, in the bath, Ken will take every opportunity there is to get you in the papers.

Then, of course, there are questionnaires. Most papers and magazines, especially teenage ones, have regular features of this type. You know the sort of thing: favourite salad dressing, most embarrassing experience with a watermelon, what colour underpants...oops, sorry, we already know that one, don't we?

Get On The Radio

Most radio stations have "playlists", lists of records the DJs and producers can choose from to play on their shows. These lists are updated during weekly playlist meetings. Each station may have several lists: A, B, C. The "C" list guaranteeing the

least plays per week and the "A" list guaranteeing
the most.

We mentioned those 200 singles released in the UK every
week. Well, Radio 1, for example, may only add about 10 of
these to their playlist each week. You'll want one of them to be
yours. This is where Chad, the "plugger", comes in.

He, like Ken, has been employed by Unigramm on a
freelance basis. His job is to try to persuade the top radio
producers and DJs to play your record.

He plays them "Cloud Cuckoo" about a
month ahead of the release date. As you're
not a well known act yet, Chad is not
finding it easy and is meeting rather a lot
of resistance, especially at Radio 1, where
they've read somewhere that you think
they're all "deaf idiots".

Doh!

However, by the end of the first week he's got you on the C
list of London's two biggest independent stations and the A list
of St Michael's Hospital Radio. Not much but it's a start and,
over the next couple of weeks, Chad will make progress with
the national stations, including Radio 1.

Caroline, who works for the same company as Chad, is
responsible for getting your record played on the independent
local radio stations around the country. A brief tour of these

stations is organised, so you pack your bags and jump in a hire car with Caroline. During the next couple of weeks you get to visit places you didn't know existed, radio stations you didn't know existed and give interviews to DJs who didn't know you existed. With a bit of luck, they'll remember you the next time they have a playlist meeting.

Get On The Telly

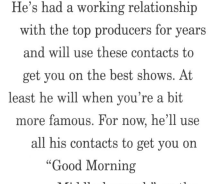

A single television appearance is worth a hundred radio plays and Bernie (Chad's partner) will be trying to get you on the telly. He's had a working relationship with the top producers for years and will use these contacts to get you on the best shows. At least he will when you're a bit more famous. For now, he'll use all his contacts to get you on "Good Morning Middlesborough" on the UK Snooze satellite channel.

Then, of course, there's your video. Bernie's been showing it to people for a few weeks now and one of the satellite music channels has already started playing it.

All the big TV producers are hedging their bets until you get a bit more radio play. Remember, there are plenty of other acts out there and they're all after the same TV slots. Most producers will go for an established act rather than take a risk with a new artist.

Go On Tour

You've built up quite a following in your local pubs and clubs over the last couple of years and now it's time to spread the word farther afield.

The live performance side of the music business has its own set of special and dedicated characters and during your first national concert tour you'll get to know and love the following:

☞ Henry, the promoter

Henry knows all the gig venues in the country, from Wembley Stadium to the Dog & Duck. He'll book the venues, deal with the ticket agencies, advertise the concerts and be ultimately responsible for collecting the dosh.

☞ Tom, the tour manager

Tom liaises with the promoter, books the hotels, organises the travel arrangements, and hires / fires all the people below, (the "crew"). He wakes you up in the morning and pushes you on stage at night. He's your nanny, your scout leader, your tour guide, your entertainment's officer, and he knows the telephone number of every Indian restaurant in the country. If you're stuck up a creek without a paddle (or Dusseldorf Airport without a passport), Tom has a speedboat waiting round the corner. (You hope.)

☞ Gaz, front of house sound engineer

You've spent the last few weeks rehearsing and the band is sounding great. This will mean nothing unless your audience can hear everything that's going on nice and clearly. Enter Gaz. He's the bloke with the headphones you see in the auditorium, standing behind all those knobs and flashing lights. He's got a similar job to Ben, the engineer in the studio. Instead of controlling what you hear on your stereo, Gaz controls what you hear over the PA (Public Address) System.

☞ Jenny, monitor engineer

It's all very well the audience hearing what you're doing, but if you can't hear yourself or the rest of the band, there'll be very little worth listening to. Jenny is in charge of the sound on stage. Each member of the band has his own set of speakers or earphones and can ask Jenny to make any other band member louder or quieter. This is constantly changing during the concert so if

you see the drummer making an inappropriate gesture to the side of the stage, he's just asking Jenny to turn the organ up.

☞ Sam, lighting designer

Sam's the other bloke with the headphones, standing next to Gaz. You may be small and insignificant...

Thank you!

...but Sam's going to make you look like a rock god. He's got moving lights, multicoloured spotlights, lasers, smoke machines, dry ice machines, film projectors and crystal balls.

Snigger!

And it's all computer controlled. He can change a desert sunset into a polar moonscape with one press of a button.

👉 Bernadette, technician

Bernie is your guitar technician (or "tech"). She looks after all your guitars and amplifiers, tunes the guitars and helps you change them during the show. Ideally, every member of the band will have their own "tech", each specialising in their particular instrument. A good tech must be able to think clearly under pressure. If something goes wrong during a show, they'll have to fix it before anyone in the audience notices.

👉 Steve, rigger

You see all those lights hanging precariously above the stage and all that stuff that looks like designer scaffolding? This is the "rig" and it's

Steve's job to get it all up there. This is accomplished using a combination of steel cable, winches, pulleys and sticky tape. He'll hang 60 feet above the stage, adjusting a spotlight with his left hand, tightening a bolt with his right and peeling a banana with his feet. Steve is, what we in the music business call, "completely barking".

Edwin & Shirley, coach drivers

Shirley drives you and the band about. Her bus is equipped with leather upholstery, air conditioning, TV, video lounge, computer games, kitchen, toilet and satellite phone. Edwin drives the crew bus. They usually travel overnight so, as well as the aforementioned equipment, this bus has bunks in it. It's a well-guarded secret what happens on the crew bus during a typical journey, but my guess is that they relax with

some nice herbal tea, read poetry to each other and, after a taxing game of I-Spy fall, exhausted but happy, into their cosy little bunks. I could be wrong.

Nicola, merchandising

If one of your adoring fans would like a tasteful souvenir to take home with them, he/she can acquire it at a very reasonable price from Nicola in the foyer. She will be selling programmes, T-shirts, sweatshirts, jackets, baseball caps, posters, postcards, blow-up dolls, plastic fruit, mugs, plates and toilet paper, all emblazoned with your wondrous, pouting countenance.

☞ Buster, security

You'll be wanting to get from the venue to your hotel without getting your clothes torn off. This is where Buster comes in. Wherever you go, he'll be about two steps behind you. He'll stop you getting hassled in clubs and mobbed in the street. He'll protect you from tabloid photographers, homicidal maniacs and hormonal girlies. His colleagues, Gnasher and Crunchie, are responsible for the safety of the band.

In addition to this, there are also truck drivers, a catering company, spotlight operators, stage builders and a local crew to help load and unload equipment.

And, if you've got more money than sense, you'll also have a wardrobe mistress, a dressing room attendant, a flower arranger and someone to test the temperature of your sushi.

And I've got more sense than money?

It would be very difficult to have less because, on your first tour, you'll be the support act for The Snot Wrestlers and won't be earning *any* money.

No money?

No, in fact, it's going to cost you a £35,000.00 "buy on" fee just for the privilege of being there.

Is it worth it?

Unigramm and Condor seem to think so, they're willing to put up the £35,000.00 between them.

They're giving me £35,000.00?

No, they're **lending** you £35,000.00. You'll pay it back out of royalties. Anyway, consider yourself lucky, there were 15 other up and coming bands after this tour and they chose you. Even after what you said about them in the papers!!

Doh!! But who's going to pay all these people you've just been talking about!

Oh, you don't have to worry! That was the Snot Wrestlers' crew. Your crew consists of Denzil, your tour manager.

Yes?

...Denzil the sound engineer, Denzil the guitar tech, Denzil the...

Er, they all seem to be called Denzil!

Yes, he's very keen and, more importantly, he's got his own van.

... And Rest!

So, when you've done all of the above, you can have a nice hot bath and a cup of Horlicks, but don't get too comfortable. That was just the United Kingdom, a mere 55 million people. There are 8 billion other people out there who've never heard of you. So, on your bike.

This is where I get to see the world?

Yep, you'll see the world all right. You'll see the TV studios of Japan, the airport lounges of the United States, the hotel rooms of Sweden, the concert halls of South America, the autobahns of Germany, the radio stations of Australia and, if you're lucky, you'll get to go up the Eiffel Tower on your day off.

Rich and Famous

Let's assume (and it's quite an assumption) that everybody went out and bought your record and you can't go anywhere without being recognised.

You're rich and famous.

Where does the money go?

Who pays for making the record?

Unigramm.

Great!

Er, but they don't give you any royalties until you've paid them back.

Oh, so I pay for the record.

That's right.

So I own the recording

Well no, they own the recording.

I pay for it and they own it.

Yep!

I see.

Who pays the producer?

You do. He'll get an advance and some of your royalty.

Who pays for the video?

This is split 50/50 between you and Unigramm.

Who pays for advertising, marketing and promotion?

Unigramm.

Who pays for the manufacture and distribution of the CD?

Unigramm but there may be a clause in your contract reducing your royalty for certain "Packaging costs", especially in the USA.

Who pays for the touring costs?

You do. And it can be a very expensive business. Unigramm may advance you money to pay rehearsal costs, band / crew wages etc. If the tour loses money (and the early ones probably will) they'll make up the difference. This is called tour support. You pay them back out of royalties.

Who pays your manager?

You do (15%-20% of everything you get, usually).

Where does the money come from? Record sales.

When some dedicated fan walks into a record shop and hands over his hard earned dosh for your album, how is this money split up? Well, that's a bit like asking how long a piece of string is.

How long is a piece of string?

It all depends on how much the record shop paid for it. If it's a big record store chain or

supermarket, they can afford to buy more records and Unigramm will give them a discount.

But, just to give you some idea, let's assume the following:

The fan pays £12.99; the record store sends £8.50 to Unigramm; Unigramm sends you £1.27$^{1}/_{2}$p.

So I get £1.27¹/₂p for every album I sell?

Yep, and your album nearly went Platinum, you sold 258,823 records.

WOW! Where's my calculator? You mean, I'll earn, wait a minute……. £329,999.32p?

Well, let's see. If I can borrow that calculator? Take away recording and video costs, tour support, advances, divide by the square root of the number you first thought of and … there we are: you owe Unigramm 68p.

What?

But it's not all bad news, Universal sends approx. 55p per album to MCPS.

Who?

The Mechanical Copyright Protection Society. Then **they** send it to the songwriter's publisher.

But, I'm the songwriter!

Exactly, so MCPS sends 55p per album, that's £142,352.65p, to Condor. They keep 30%, take off your advances and give you the rest. You pay Simon his share and end up, after three years' work, with the princely sum of £59,717.48p. Better than a slap on the bum with a rotten cucumber but hardly enough for the Ferrari.

Told you you'd have to be good at sums.

Performance Royalties

There are, however, other sources of income. For example, every time "Cloud Cuckoo" is played on the radio, the radio station has to pay an agreed amount of money to PRS.

Who?

That's the Performing Rights Society. They then send 50% straight to the songwriter (you) and 50% to the writer's publisher (Condor). Then, under the terms of your publishing contract, Condor send 40% of that money to you.

My brain hurts!

The bigger the radio station's audience, the more they pay. The same goes for TV companies and anyone else who plays music in public. Even when you play your own songs during a concert, a small percentage of the ticket revenue goes straight to the PRS.

Merchandising and Endorsements

We've already mentioned those T-shirts and posters or

"merchandising". If you're successful, there'll be many companies offering to handle your merchandising. They'll pay a flat fee for the exclusive rights to your photographs or offer a royalty per item sold. The "items" can range from Duncan Donut bubblebath to Duncan Donut donuts.

You may also get approached by companies offering "endorsements". You could appear in a TV commercial, drinking a can of Pukey Cola, for instance. In return, you get huge wads of fivers, as much Pukey Cola as you can drink or the company will sponsor your next concert tour. You, of course, refuse on the grounds that it might compromise your artistic integrity.

Er?

Tour Revenue

As we've already mentioned, you're unlikely to earn anything on your first few tours. Indeed, as you found out with the Snot Wrestlers, you can lose an awful lot of money.

If you're playing in front of 50,000 people each night, you'll earn money. Large portions on merchandising alone. But, with smaller or medium sized venues, you'll find it very difficult to cover your costs, let alone make a profit.

DUNCAN'S DIARY

(Two days in the life of a pop megastar).

A good famous day

Tuesday 14th

8.30am *Wake up, refreshed in my luxury hotel suite. Light breakfast in room. Buster (security) arrives to carry my bags to the limo. Take the scenic route through Rome, past the Colosseum to the airport.*

9.45am *A few fans waiting at the airport. Pose for photos, sign a few autographs. All very polite. Makes me feel good to see their shining faces. Buster checks me in and we're whisked away on one of those golf trolleys to the VIP lounge. Free champagne and munchies. Great flight, stewardesses couldn't do enough for me, more autographs etc.*

11.55am *Limo picks us up from airport and drives us into London. Read papers on the way. Fantastic review in PQ Magazine. "Duncan Donut's genius is on show as never before in this, the most exciting album of the decade *****".*

1.15pm *Lunch at Pierre Le Ponce's with the gorgeous Sophie from The Daily Globe. The best table, overlooking the park. I have the duck with the crème caramel to follow. Delicious.*

Interview was good too. We got into some really deep stuff, not your usual tabloid pap. Quite a flirt, is Sophie.

3.00pm *Pop round the corner with Buster to buy a few clothes. They close the shop for me so I don't get any hassle. Get this cool Ted Smith jacket. Would've been £800 but Ted happened to be in the shop and gave it to me "to wear it to a few high profile parties", he said.*

4.30pm *Arrive at the gig for soundcheck. Band already there. Three interviews to do and there's a TV crew here from MTV to do a "fly on the wall thing". All goes well, I seem to be on a roll today.*

6.15pm *Grab a light meal and forty winks before the show.*

9.00pm *On stage. What a gig! What a rush! What an audience. 17,000 of them. And all there to see me. Sound was great too. Straight off stage and into the limo. Hotel to freshen up before the party.*

12.45am *Arrive at Swanky's for the after show party. Anybody who's anybody is there. All my celebrity chums and their celebrity chums. Paparazzi are out in force. Police have to stop the traffic to get me in. Everybody wants to talk to me, tell me how great the show was. Have a few cocktails and a lot of laughs.*

5.15am *Back at hotel I fall, blissfully, into bed. I'm great, me.*

Self esteem rating: 98.6%

<u>A not so good famous day</u>

Wednesday 15th

6.30am Awoken (in my luxury hotel suite) by three alarm calls and Buster banging on the door. Someone broke in during the night, drilled holes in my head, filled it with barbed wire, plastered my eyelids shut and carpeted the inside of my mouth. No time for breakfast. Buster carries my bags (and me) downstairs and throws us both into a minicab. Pursued down street by hotel employee shouting something about a missing toilet seat.

7.15am Stuck in traffic. We'll never catch that plane. Read the papers to try and take my mind off my hangover. Wish I hadn't. Lousy reviews of last night's show. "Sounded like a cat having it's stomach pumped", Bernard Bernardson, The Echo. "Not quite as much fun as having an ingrown toenail removed", Walter Witt, The London Herald. And, to top it all, the "gorgeous" Sophie thinks I'm "boring and self obsessed".

8.30am Arrive at airport. Usual fans are there again. How do they know where I'm going to be before I do? What do they all want from me?

Simon and the band are inside, waiting. Luckily, the plane has been delayed an hour so I can relax a bit. At least, I could if that rugby team would stop laughing and pointing at me and that freelance photographer would naff off. Oh no, I've been spotted by a bunch of Spanish school kids. Help!

9.05am Nightmare flight. They've screwed the seats up and I'm sitting next to a shower curtain salesman from Gillingham. He seems to think he's my best mate or something. Keeps asking for my address so he can send me his brother's demo.

Haven't eaten since last night. The airport café wouldn't take Danish Kroner. The in flight "meal" arrives and it's sausage and bacon, which would be very nice if I wasn't a vegetarian. "We might be able to find you a carrot", the steward suggests, helpfully.

11.30am (German time) Arrive at Dusseldorf airport. Stopped by customs. Next 45 mins with Brunhilda rummaging through my smalls.

12.15pm Eventually released into the Arrivals lounge to pandemonium. People pushing, shouting, flash guns going off, police trying to keep order. All this for me? Actually, no. Some Russian tennis player. What a relief. Though I could do with a bit of attention... Hello? Over here? Do you know who I am? Self obsessed? Me? Wait 'til I see the "gorgeous" Sophie again.

12.20pm Greeted by a very flustered Gunter, from Unigramm Germany. Already running 2 hours late. TV crew from a local station expecting to do an in-depth interview right

now. We've been told nothing about it. Furious argument ensues between Simon & Gunter. End up in the multi-storey car park doing a, not so, in-depth interview and answering questions like "How does it feel to be in Dusseldorf", with a forced smile and a couple of words of German.

12.45pm Before we can get on the coach, have to negotiate a barricade of 30 dubious looking characters with assorted anoraks and comedy moustaches. They're armed to the teeth with felt pens of various colours, stacks of blank white card and the most embarrassing photographs of me ever taken. These are the professional "Autogram" hunters and nothing will stop them getting my signature. As if from some invisible signal, they pounce like sharks on an injured tuna. My pathetic pleas go unheeded "Just one each, guys", "We're running a bit late, got to go now". Resistance is futile.

Fortunately Gunter has started to fear for his job. We should've been at the stadium an hour ago to rehearse tonight's TV show and the director's on the mobile chewing his ear off. In desperation, he attacks the left flank whilst Buster swoops in from the right, scooping me up and throwing me on the coach. They quickly follow, the doors hiss shut and we're on our way.

12.50pm Having just collapsed into my seat, I'm informed that the celebrity columnist for the biggest national newspaper is on board along with his trusty photographer and they're "ready for the interview now!" Turns out, this is on the schedule, Simon knew all about it but didn't have the heart to tell me. Nothing on the coach but beer. Boy, am I hungry.

2.00pm Arrive at stadium. One of those big TV pop festivals they have over here. Loads of big bands from all over the place miming their biggest hits. The place will be packed tonight. 22,000 people. Shown into grey concrete bunker somewhere in the depths of the stadium. It's about 5 metres square with no window, a bench seat, a mirror and a toilet/shower.

Informed by rather attractive lady in leather trousers, with leather clipboard and leather headphones, that we've missed our rehearsal slot but must wait here in case the director can fit us in later. We've also missed lunch but she'll see if she can rustle us up a few sandwiches.

4.30pm No sign of director or sandwiches. Everyone else has disappeared to the hospitality area. It's full of young, trendy beautiful people looking for someone famous to pounce on. All the "pouncees" are probably cowering in their dressing rooms like me. Besides, I've got some interviews to do.

5.25pm Try to get some kip but these benches aren't exactly comfortable. I miss Jane (girlfriend). Haven't seen her for six weeks and she couldn't make the London show. The guys in the band are great but we've been virtually living together for the last month and we're sick of the sight of each other.

6.00pm Desperate search for food. Can't find anything without a sausage in it. Eventually track down some boiled cabbage marinated in disinfectant. Supposed to be a delicacy in these parts.

6.15pm Wish I hadn't eaten that cabbage. Feel worse than I did before. Leather-clad clipboard lady turns up again. We're not going to get a rehearsal after all.

Two quick telephone interviews to promote a gig we're doing in Sweden tomorrow.

7.30pm Have some make-up slapped on. Back to the bunker. Stage clothes on and more hanging about.

8.15pm On stage. Ready to mime Cloud Cuckoo and they start playing Love and Porridge by Conan Bleating. Stand there like idiots until they realise what's happening and stop the tape. Embarrassed silence, nervous whistling from the crowd. Suddenly, Cloud Cuckoo starts from about halfway through the second verse and we join in as though nothing has happened. Midway through the second chorus, the camera zooms in, I look to my left and realise that the day is lost. Live on German National TV, I am performing a duet with a man dressed as a giant chicken. We leave the stage to the sound of bewildered murmuring.

9.00pm We cut our losses and escape the venue before the show ends. Unfortunately, neither security nor the coach driver are ready for us and we find ourselves in the

middle of about 200 screaming fans. Things start getting ugly and, by the time security arrives, my Ted Smith jacket is in tatters, my left eye is black, my lip is bleeding and my bag is missing. Three girls and a boy are taken to hospital with minor injuries.

I eventually make it to the coach and wonder what would've happened if they didn't like me!

9.30pm Back to hotel. Quick shower and out to try and find somewhere to get my first meal of the day. More fans in front of the hotel, so we escape through the kitchens. Everywhere booked up. End up in an Italian restaurant in the middle of nowhere. At least it's quiet. Gunter full of apologies. Feel sorry for him.

Halfway through my tagliatelle, a guy comes over and insists on his two daughters having their photograph taken with me. I grin and bear it until he "instructs" me to give them both a kiss, at which point I lose it and launch into a major rant, "what am I, a performing seal"? etc. A scene ensues and we're politely asked to leave.

11.15pm Find a bar in the east of the city. Seems pretty mellow. Alas, no. Some girl wants an autograph. Drunk, jealous boyfriend wants a fight. Buster steps in and cools things down but lose my appetite for adventure and retreat to the hotel.

12.20am Fall into bed watching a German documentary on ice fishing. At least I might get a few hours sleep tonight. Another early start tomorrow. Sweden. Doh! Wasn't my passport in the bag I lost?

I'm rubbish, me.

Self esteem rating: 4.2%

So, after a day like that, you may be wondering why you're doing this.

Why am I doing this?

Because you're driven to do it. You can't help yourself. It's what you do and you'll suffer as many Wednesday 15ths as you have to, just to get one more Tuesday 14th.

You're hooked and nothing can save you now, you drift into a deep, dark sleep and wake to find Mr Yawn drumming his fingers on your desk. He seems none too pleased.

"Well?" he hisses through his teeth, "I say again, how long is a rat's colon?"

Keep practising!!